DEATH
Program of Programs

CHARLES MWEWA

Copyright © 2024 Charles Mwewa

www.charlesmwewa.com

Published by:

ACP

Ottawa, ON Canada

www.acpress.ca

www.spirngopus.com

Email:

info@acpress.ca

All rights reserved.

ISBN: 978-1-998788-73-6

DEDICATION

To and for all.
Because we shall all die.

CONTENTS

DEDICATION iii
CONTENTS v
AUTHOR'S WORD vii

1 | INEVITABILITY OF DEATH 1
   Preoccupation 1
   Preparation 2
      Spiritual preparation 2
      Financial preparation 3
      Social or moral preparation 4
   Presentation 6
   Conclusion 9

2 | INVIOLABILITY OF LIFE 11
   Sacred in Nature 11
   Sacred in Nurture 12
   Sacred in Culture 12
   Conclusion 14

3 | IRREVOCABILITY OF GOOD BEHAVIOR . 15
   The Unsustainability of Human Pride 16
   The Insolvability of the Death Trap 17

The Irrevocability of Right Living..............................18
Conclusion...19
ABOUT THE AUTHOR...21
SELECTED BOOKS BY THIS AUTHOR..........23
INDEX..29

AUTHOR'S WORD

Death is the surest program that always happens. It's inevitable. It is inexorable. It is inviolable. It is incorrigible. And it is irrevocable. Thus, death is unavoidable and predictable. We may not know the day and time we will die, but we know that we shall die. For this reason, death must be the most important program of every individual on earth – young, adults, and the elderly.

1 | INEVITABILITY OF DEATH

When something is inevitable, it is bound to happen, no matter what happens. Therefore, death will happen. And because of this, it requires the following three factors: Preoccupation; preparation; and presentation.

Preoccupation

We must be preoccupied with the thinking, feeling and speaking on and about death. Human general attitude has been avoidance. Avoidance to talking about death seems like a defensive mechanism. But it is only postponing troubles. There are also myths associated to discussing death. Some think that if they talk about death, then it will come, sort of "talk about the death, and he shows up" thing. Well, he may not show up or he will show up. But eventually, he shall show up. So, talking or thinking about it, is just inevitable.

Since death is either the final friend or fiend, it calls for dutiful preoccupation. Everyone will meet it in the final analysis, but it's better to meet it well-prepared. That is why the next inevitability is preparation.

Preparation

We are certain to meet death one day, and that is the reason why we must be prepared to meet it. Death will happen. Preparation must include the following three areas: spiritual; financial; social or moral.

Spiritual preparation

Since by definition, death is the absence of the soul from the body, it, therefore, follows that we get to the spiritual end of our living with knowledge. We cannot simply die and then become aware of our demise *post facto*; we must, rather, get involved with it before it happens.

Fortunately, religion provides an avenue for spiritual preparation. It is amazing that every moral and spiritual leader, including Jesus Christ, Mohammed, Buddha, Confucius, etc., have written and taught extensively on the topic of death. What we call the "Day of Judgment," is simply an allusion to the need for preparation for death spiritually. It is not the author's objective to show the reader how to get spiritually ready for death in this book. Readers may refer or consult their own religious or moral leaders for that. It is, however, suffice to note that any aspect of spiritual preparation for death must involve some theoretical or philosopher postulation on the importance of a clean and purified soul. This motif runs across religious underpinnings.

Financial preparation

Whether one dies expectantly or unexpectantly, death is expensive. There is no free death anymore. Even those who contemplate suicide must consider the financial implication of their own death. There is no nation on earth, and no individual on the globe exempted from this requirement. Death requires financial or pecuniary preparation. Coffins are expensive, so are cemeteries and funeral processions. Death needs financial preparedness.

Social or moral preparation

Family, friends and relatives become involved in the death of their loved ones. The important moral question, however, is how well or rightly did one live? Death cannot simply be brushed away in life; it has moral implications. To die good, we must live good.

But the greatest social preparedness we must think about before we die is the impact of our death on those we live behind. Have you ever wondered the reason why in every culture and society people have an erroneous view that the dead listen? Well, they may not. Their vacation on earth may as well have ended at their death. They may not listen or hear us. It could merely be a myth, a belief imbued in fear and the unknown that people think that the dead are here among us.

For example, the dead can't say, "Thank you," no matter how many flowers we place on their graves. They will not nod a "yes" no matter how many adulations we heap on their character or achievements. They are dead. Period. But why do we still honor, heap them with praise or place expensive wreaths and bouquets on their memorials, you may ask? We do it for the living. We know that those who are still living are watching us, and implicitly, we try to ingratiate ourselves with the memory of the dead by punning to the living's silent demands.

Therefore, gratitude is for the living, including those who have helped us, assisted us, cared for us, provided for us, defended us or loved us. We must take inventory of the people who have meant so much in our lives – rewarding them with, "Thank yous," before we die. They will need to hear it before they die, too. Not after they are dead. They will not hear it or know about it.

Gratitude should not always be with money – that is engineered gratification. True gratitude is with kind, meaningful and heart-felt words or actions. It can be followed up by things, but that is conditional upon how much one has. Because it doesn't depend on money or things, everyone can be grateful and show gratitude before they die.

Our Merciful Lord said, "Let the dead bury the dead." An English proverb says, "Charity begins at home." And a spiritual philosopher said, "Let us do good unto all men, especially unto them who are of the household of faith."

We cannot, thus, be grateful to outsiders before we are grateful to those around us, in our homes, churches, mosques, synagogues, temples, palaces, clubs, teams, or places of work. Before we die, we must remember to be grateful and to say, "Thank you," often, to our spouses, children, parents, friends, and even enemies. That will be true social and moral preparation.

Rule of thumb – be grateful and thankful to the living – because they will appreciate and honor it.

Presentation

Many people are concerned about how they will be presented in death. And they are right. In this modern time, this is a legitimate concern. As it was alluded to earlier, death is costly. People desire that their sense of dignity will be maintained in death as it was in life. In short, how they are presented at and in death, is very important to them.

When we are alive, we cleaned up ourselves, we protected our secrets and confidences. But when we die, someone else must do that for us.

And in this world of social media and technology, we may find ourselves open for discussions. We may not be able to have protected important information about us and our confidences.

While God will be dealing, spiritually, with our spirits and souls, it is human beings who will be handling our bodies. Our dignity, thus, is in question, even in death. Of course, we may not be there, and that more the reason why we need to think about how we shall be presented in death. For this, some have written down wills (testates), and hired lawyers and administrators to manage their estates.

Human dignity is paramount both in life and in death. There are four reasons why we must protect our humanity, with dignity and respect, even in death.

First, because our humanity is us. We are human and that is reason enough for everyone around us to respect us and treat us with dignity. There is no other reason before it. If we have to look for other reasons, they should be supplementary, not definitive. We are human, and that is enough to warrant respect and kind treatment from all, in life and in death.

Second, because we are important just because we are us. This is a supplementary reason but it relates to the first one. We are important and valuable just because we are we – with everything we are and have or had. We must not go out of our way to be different. Just the way we are, we are vital and important. If we must improve, it is not to be "another" but we improve within the understanding that we are improving us, our very best original. Even in death, no-one should think less of us, no matter what they discover about us.

Third, because our value is not relative to anyone or anything. We are human and important, even in death. No-one and nobody should require us to meet anybody's standard. There is nothing like that. We are our own standard. We are exactly what we should be – no matter what others think. We should be treated, our bodies, too, with dignity in death even when we are unconscious. Our appearance and presentation must be treated with honor and the sacredness they deserve.

So, our bodies must be protected, and our nakedness should not be subjected to ignominy and humiliation. Our final appearance must be given the best salute and make-up and our general aura should be that of a grandiose send-off. Our funerals must be well-planned and our caskets, clothing, and choice of veneers, all must meet a crescendo in grand finale of our life – as if we died on top of the world.

Fourth, because nobody is better than us. Anyone who claims to be better or worthier than us is not credible. Some people may believe that they are better than others, but that is just a belief. The truth is that we are the best in ourselves, our kind, make, personality, behavior, etc. We should not be the one who changes to suit others. Rather, if they want, let others change to suit us. Otherwise, as we have respect and dignity for others, so should they for us. We are important. We have intrinsic value peculiar only to us. And we are worthy in ourselves. When we are alive, we should not lose sleep because someone else told us that we were substandard. That is and was their opinion.

Conclusion

Rule of thumb – we are valuable, and we deserve respect and dignity from all, in life and when we die. However, our own thoughts and actions before we died are important. If we can, we should die with wills. And even if we die intestate, there are laws that protect the sanctity and dignity of the dead. Death must not be an after-thought for the living, because it is inevitable. And its inevitability means that it will require preoccupation, preparation, and presentation.

2 | INVIOLABILITY OF LIFE

We cannot honor death if we did not honor life. We must think and do everything possible to die a good death by living right. The two go hand in hand. A good life presupposes a good death. Life is sacred. Here are three inviolables of life: sacred in nature; sacred in nurture; and sacred in culture.

Sacred in Nature

Our human sacredness comes innately – it is not a product of our environment. It is inherent in us at birth, beginning at conception. A fetus may look defenceless, but think about it this way. At some point in time, you were that fetus. Now think again, if someone decided for you to be terminated or violated, in your defenceless state. And think about millions of babies who are being murdered and maimed by irresponsible adult decisions. Life is sacred, and human life must be protected from conception.

Sacred in Nurture

Humanity must grow up with respect and dignity as explained in Chapter 1. But people's upbringing must be such that they are pointed to a better ending. Children must know from early years that they must be good and live right. They must be groomed to be morally upright and intellectually sustaining. They must be made aware that they are a gift of life and that thinking they must pass on to the generations after them. Human beings must be raised up in an environment that respects human life and respects and honors human death.

Sacred in Culture

Culture defines a person's values, ethos,

principles, basically their way of living – from birth to death. It is all they are and society has a lot to do with a person's culture. Our culture can be anything but negligent of the end of life should not be one of it. People should be free to think, to innovate, to manipulate anything for the good of all, etc. But people should not advocate for the desecration of life and the violation of the sacredness of death. Culture must uphold the inviolability of life and death.

Sacred in culture also means that we must dispose of the death with honor and respect. Cemeteries must be chosen intelligently, guarded militantly, and decorated beautifully. People's last resting places should be more grandiose than even when they lived. Some might think that there is hypocrisy in that. There is not. When people are alive, they are subjected to social competition – competition for scarce resources, etc. When they are alive, they have capabilities and competencies. But when they die, they become permanently incapacitated. They have zero capacity. The collective effort of the living should ensure that they are sent off well and respectably.

Conclusion

What we do in life should be reflected in death. The purity of life must be reflected in the dignity of death. Those who are alive have a responsibility to ensuring that the dead are honored. Every dead body (corpse) must be buried, for example. Every buried dead body must be registered. And every registered dead body must be protected. Those who are cremated, must be subjected to ethical and environmentally accepted standards. Their ashes must be respectably preserved and dispatched.

3 | IRREVOCABILITY OF GOOD BEHAVIOR

Death may not be directly defeated, but it can be indirectly. The strength of death is bad behavior. In fact, in mythologies and religions, death came in response to offence or moral decay or sin. The genesis of death also seems to be disobedience to divine precepts. In human terms, we assign the stiffest penalties to the death row. The assumption is that, and this is humanly understandable, death is harshest sentence in life. When people die, implicitly, we assume that they are paying the ultimate price. There are three aspects of the irrevocability of good behavior: The Unsustainability of Human Pride; The Insolvability of the Death Trap; and The Irrevocability of Right Living.

The Unsustainability of Human Pride

Every human being has thought about death in a way you may not expect. They have thought about a supposition that they lived forever. They have contemplated, or even attempted to sustain that thought, but only to be disappointed because they see everyone dying – their loved ones, relatives, friends and foes. Death is contrary to reason. There is no facet of the human brain that accepts or even sustains it. That is why, the thought of death is an afterthought.

Death automatically triggers sorrow. This happens because humans have no capacity to defeat death. Death leaves the living hopeless – hopeless that they cannot hop, at least, in the interim, for the defeat of death. Even die-hard Christian believers cry when loved ones die, even when they know that God will resurrect them. Jesus Himself wept[1] at Lazarus's tomb.

---

[1] John 11:35

Death brings paralysis to human pride. It challenges man's intelligence. The brutal and rude reality is that the best among the humans are only humans at best. The meaning is that however powerful they may seem in human judgment (great thinkers, extremely wealthy, holders of political or social influence, etc.), they will die. When it comes to death, it is an equalizer; the best and worst will die, and so are the righteous and the wicked. The rich die, so do the poor. Smart people die, so do the dull and the not-so-smart people. No-one wins with death. It crashes human pride.

The Insolvability of the Death Trap

God and gods have given their final verdict on death – it will not go out of the earth until everyone dies. Everyone will taste death. It is a trap, and everyone will be caught into it – the capable and the uncapable, the wise and the foolish. It is a necessary menace and it prides in its ability to capture anyone it feels like taking.

Humans may be good at setting traps for other animals, but even Albert Einstein died. Death is a mockery; it mocks those who claim to be the greatest in human sphere, and it mocks those who invent medicines to cure incurable diseases. The trap can be postponed and even eluded, sometimes, but it eventually triggers. That is the insolvability of the death trap.

The Irrevocability of Right Living

Death, no matter how powerful it can be, cannot permanently defeat right living. Right tramps over death. It may be shocking to many that there is life after death, that is because death has no permanently victory. But there is a catch, to enjoy permanent victory over death, one must invest in rightness.[2]

Right living is not only a preparation for life, it is also a preparation for death. The best way to prepare for death is to be ready to love other people in life. Since death will come, it must be the first priority of every human being to make love a life goal. When we love one another, we will also love and respect their Creator, and we will do to them exactly what we want them to do to us. Because when we love, we laugh at death. It may get us, but it will never have us.

---

[22] See this author's book, *Moral Capitalism: The Critical Examination of the Concept of Rightness in the Context of Human Goodness* (ACP: Ottawa, 2024).

DEATH
Program of Programs

Conclusion

The author ends this chapter, and this book, with a poem called "Death, Sweeter,"

> They say that death is always bad
> I say, nada, it isn't always that sad
> In fact, it can be even saner, sweeter
> For it can be, too, opposite of bitter
> The meat you ate today, was dead
> And the chicken for lunch also bled
> Things that give life, come from death
> Milk we drink, from cows without breath,
> Eggs we scramble, were first expired
> To live long, from death we are inspired
> And that envious way to sweet heaven
> Via death it passes to our blissful haven
> O death, fear we not if at our right time
> But loathe we you deathly if at our prime.

ABOUT THE AUTHOR

Award-Winning, Best-Selling Author, Charles Mwewa (LLB; BA Law; BA Ed; LLM), is a prolific researcher, poet, novelist, lawyer, law professor and Christian apologist and intercessor. Mwewa has written no less than 100 books and counting in every genre and has exhibited his works at prestigious expos like the Ottawa International Book Expo and is the winner of the Coppa Awards for his signature publication, *Zambia: Struggles of My People*.
Mwewa and his family live in the Canadian Capital City of Ottawa.

SELECTED BOOKS BY THIS AUTHOR

1. *ZAMBIA: Struggles of My People (First and Second Editions)*
2. *10 FINANCIAL & WEALTH ATTITUDES TO AVOID*
3. *10 STRATEGIES TO DEFEAT STRESS AND DEPRESSION: Creating an Internal Safeguard against Stress and Depression*
4. *100+ REASONS TO READ BOOKS*
5. *A CASE FOR AFRICA?S LIBERTY: The Synergistic Transformation of Africa and the West into First-World Partnerships*
6. *DECOLONIZATION: Reclaiming African Originality and Destiny*
7. *A PANDEMIC POETRY, COVID-19*
8. *ALLERGIC TO CORRUPTION: The Legacy of President Michael Sata of Zambia*
9. *BOOK ABOUT SOMETHING: On Ultimate Purpose*
10. *CAMPAIGN FOR AFRICA: A Provocative Crusade for the Economic and Humanitarian Decolonization of Africa*
11. *CHAMPIONS: Application of Common Sense and Biblical Motifs to Succeed in Both Worlds*
12. *CORONAVIRUS PRAYERS*
13. *HH IS THE RIGHT MAN FOR ZAMBIA: And Other Acclaimed Articles on Zambia and Africa*
14. *I BOW: 3500 Prayer Lines of Inspiration & Intercession from the Heart: Volume One*
15. *INTERUNIVERSALISM IN A NUTSHELL: For Iranian Refugee Claimants*
16. *LAW & GRACE: An Expository Study in the Rudiments of Sin and Truth*
17. *LAWS OF INFLUENCE: 7even Lessons in*

Transformational Leadership
18. LOVE IDEAS IN COVID PANDEMIC TIMES: *For Couples & Lovers*
19. P.A.S.S: *Version 2: Answer Bank*
20. P.A.S.S.: *Acing the Ontario Paralegal-Licensing Examination, Version 2*
21. POETRY: *The Best of Charles Mwewa*
22. QUOT-EBOS: *Essential. Barbs. Opinions. Sayings*
23. REASONING WITH GOD IN PRAYER: *Poetic Verses for Peace & Unconfronted Controversies*
24. RESURRECTION: *(A Spy in Hell Novel)*
25. I DREAM OF AFRICA: *Poetry of Post-Independence Africa, the Case of Zambia*
26. SERMONS: *Application of Legal Principles and Procedures in the Life and Ministry of Christ*
27. SONG OF AN ALIEN: *Over 130 Poems of Love, Romance, Passion, Politics, and Life in its Complexity*
28. TEMPORARY RESIDENCE APPLICATION
29. THE GRACE DEVOTIONAL: *Fifty-two Happy Weeks with God*
30. THE SYSTEM: *How Society Defines & Confines Us: A Worksheet*
31. FAIRER THAN GRACE: *My Deepest for His Highest*
32. WEALTH THINKING: *And the Concept of Capisolism*
33. PRAYER: *All Prayer Makes All Things Possible*
34. PRAYER: *All Prayer Makes All Things Possible, Answers*
35. PRISONER OF GRACE: *An I Saw Jesus at Milton Vision*
36. PRAYERS OF OUR CHILDREN
37. TEN BASIC LESSONS IN PRAYER
38. VALLEY OF ROSES: *City Called Beautiful*
39. THE PATCH THEOREM: *A Philosophy of Death, Life and Time*

40. *50 RULES OF POLITICS: A Rule Guide on Politics*
41. *ALLERGIC TO CORRUPTION: The Legacy of President Michael Sata of Zambia*
42. *INTRODUCTION TO ZAMBIAN ENVIRONMENTAL LEGISLATIVE SCHEME*
43. *REFUGEE PROTECTION IN CANADA: For Iranian Christian Convert Claimants*
44. *LAW & POVERTY (unpublished manuscript)*
45. *CHRISTIAN CONTROVERSIES: Loving Homosexuals*
46. *THINKING GOVERNMENT: Principles & Predilections*
47. *WHY MARRIED COUPLES LIE TO EACH OTHER: A Treatise*
48. *LOVE & FRIENDSHIP TIPS FOR GEN Z*
49. *POVERTY DISCOURSE: Spiritual Imperative or Social Construct*
50. *SEX BEFORE WEDDING: The Tricky Trilemma*
51. *QUOTABLE QUOTES EXCELLENCE, VOL. 1: Knowledge & Secrets*
52. *QUOTABLE QUOTES EXCELLENCE, VOL. 2: Love & Relationships*
53. *QUOTABLE QUOTES EXCELLENCE, VOL. 3: Hope*
54. *QUOTABLE QUOTES EXCELLENCE, VOL. 4: Justice, Law & Morality*
55. *QUOTABLE QUOTES EXCELLENCE, VOL. 5: Dreams & Vision*
56. *QUOTABLE QUOTES EXCELLENCE, VOL. 6: Character & Perseverance*
57. *QUOTABLE QUOTES EXCELLENCE, VOL. 7: Actions*
58. *QUOTABLE QUOTES EXCELLENCE, 1 of 20: Knowledge & Secrets*
59. *QUOTABLE QUOTES EXCELLENCE, 2 of 20: Love & Relationships*

60. *QUOTABLE QUOTES EXCELLENCE, 3 of 20: Hope*
61. *QUOTABLE QUOTES EXCELLENCE, 4 of 20: Justice, Law & Morality*
62. *QUOTABLE QUOTES EXCELLENCE, 5 of 20: Vision & Dreams*
63. *THE SEVEN LAWS OF LOVE*
64. *THE BURDEN OF ZAMBIA*
65. *BEMBA DYNASTY I (1 of a Trilogy)*
66. *BEMBA DYNASTY II (2 of a Trilogy)*
67. *ETHICAL MENTORSHIP: Missing Link in Transformational Leadership*
68. *AFRICA MUST BE DEVELOPED: Agenda for the 22nd Century Domination*
69. *INNOVATION: The Art of Starting Something New*
70. *TOWARDS TRUE ACHIEVEMENT: The Mundane & the Authentic*
71. ONE WORLD UNDER PRAYER: *For Camerron, Ecuador, and France*
72. ONE WORLD UNDER PRAYER: *For New Zealand, Poland, and Uganda*
73. ONE WORLD UNDER PRAYER: *For Malta, USA, and Zambia*
74. ONE WORLD UNDER PRAYER: *For Germany*
75. ONE WORLD UNDER PRAYER: *For Haiti, Iraq, and Russia*
76. ONE WORLD UNDER PRAYER: *For Chad, UN, and Syria*
77. ONE WORLD UNDER PRAYER: *For Burundi, Canada, and Israel*
78. ONE WORLD UNDER PRAYER: *For China, Egypt, and Venezuela*
79. ONE WORLD UNDER PRAYER: *For Greece, Mali, and Ukraine*

DEATH
Program of Programs

80. *ONE WORLD UNDER PRAYER: For Morocco, North Korea, and the UK*
81. *ONE WORLD UNDER PRAYER: For Belgium, Brazil, and the Burkina Faso*
82. *ADIEU PERFECTIONS: A Satire*
83. *OPTIMIZATION: Turning Low Moments into High Comments*
84. *ACING THE IMPOSSIBLE: Faith in the Other Dimension*
85. *END GAME LAW: Financial Mindset in Quotables*
86. *MARRIAGE MAPPING METHODOLOGY: The Outline of How to Measure the Strength, Love-Condition and Longevity of a Marriage*
87. *A CASE AGAINST WAR: The Imperative of Love and the Unsustainability of Peace*
88. *BORROW TO GROW: Accessing Other's Achievements to Your Benefit*
89. *WESTERN CHRISTIANITY NEVER BEEN PURE: A Treatise*
90. *MISERABLE UNSAVING: A Poetic Satire on Money Mindset for Non-Saving Upbringings*
91. *MORAL CAPTALISM: The Critical Examination of the Concept of Rightness in the Context of Human Goodness*
92. *POETRY OF CHARISTMAS: How Holy and Jolly the Night Jesus Christ was Born*
93. *REJECTION: The Perfect Path to Perfection, A Treatise*
94. *MONEY: All about the Exchange*
95. *DEATH: Program of Programs*

INDEX

A

adults, vii
Africa, 23, 24
Albert Einstein, 17
avoidance, 1

B

behavior, 9, 15
Buddha. *See* spiritual
 leader

C

Christian, 21
Confucius. *See* spiritual
 leader

D

Death, vii
Death Trap, v, 16, 17
Death, Sweeter. *See* poem

E

elderly, vii

equalizer, 17

F

financial. *See* three areas
friend, 2

G

God, 7, 16, 17, 24

H

human judgment, 17
Human Pride, v, 16

I

incorrigible. *See* Death
inevitable. *See* Death
inexorable. *See* Death
inviolable. *See* Death
irrevocable. *See* Death

J

Jesus Christ. *See* spiritual
 leader

L

law, 21
lawyer, 21
Lazarus, 16
love, 18

M

Mohammed. *See* spiritual leader

P

poem, 19
predictable. *See* Death
preoccupation. *See* three factors
preparation. *See* three factors
presentation. *See* three factors
professor, 21
program. *See* Death
prolific, 21

R

Right Living, vi, 16, 18
rightness, 18

S

sacred in culture. *See* three inviolables of life
sacred in nature. *See* three inviolables of life
sacred in nurture. *See* three inviolables of life
social or moral. *See* three areas
spiritual. *See* three areas
spiritual leader, 3
Struggles of My People, 21, 23

T

testates. *See* will
the West, 23
three areas, 2
three factors, 1
three inviolables of life, 11

U

unavoidable. *See* Death

W

will, 7

DEATH
Program of Programs

Y

Z

young, vii

Zambia, 21, 23, 24, 25

www.ingramcontent.com/pod-product-compliance
Lightning Source LLC
Chambersburg PA
CBHW070751050426
42449CB00010B/2430